OCEAN LIFE UP CLOSE

Eels

by Nathan Sommer

BLASTOFF! READERS

3

BELLWETHER MEDIA · MINNEAPOLIS, MN

Note to Librarians, Teachers, and Parents:

Blastoff! Readers are carefully developed by literacy experts and combine standards-based content with developmentally appropriate text.

Level 1 provides the most support through repetition of high-frequency words, light text, predictable sentence patterns, and strong visual support.

Level 2 offers early readers a bit more challenge through varied simple sentences, increased text load, and less repetition of high-frequency words.

Level 3 advances early-fluent readers toward fluency through increased text and concept load, less reliance on visuals, longer sentences, and more literary language.

Level 4 builds reading stamina by providing more text per page, increased use of punctuation, greater variation in sentence patterns, and increasingly challenging vocabulary.

Level 5 encourages children to move from "learning to read" to "reading to learn" by providing even more text, varied writing styles, and less familiar topics.

Whichever book is right for your reader, Blastoff! Readers are the perfect books to build confidence and encourage a love of reading that will last a lifetime!

This edition first published in 2018 by Bellwether Media, Inc.

No part of this publication may be reproduced in whole or in part without written permission of the publisher. For information regarding permission, write to Bellwether Media, Inc., Attention: Permissions Department, 5357 Penn Avenue South, Minneapolis, MN 55419.

Library of Congress Cataloging-in-Publication Data

Names: Sommer, Nathan, author.
Title: Eels / by Nathan Sommer.
Description: Minneapolis, MN : Bellwether Media, Inc., [2018] | Series: Blastoff! Readers. Ocean Life Up Close | Audience: K to Grade 3. | Includes bibliographical references and index.
Identifiers: LCCN 2017028811 | ISBN 9781626177659 (hardcover : alk. paper) | ISBN 9781681034744 (ebook)
Subjects: LCSH: Eels–Juvenile literature.
Classification: LCC QL637.9.A5 S66 2018 | DDC 597/.43–dc23
LC record available at https://lccn.loc.gov/2017028811

Editor: Paige V. Polinsky   Designer: Brittany McIntosh

Printed in the United States of America, North Mankato, MN.

Table of Contents

giant
moray eel

Eels are fish that look like snakes.
They use their long, thin bodies to
slither through the sea!

There are more than 800 types of eels. All are fierce **predators**.

fimbriated
moray eel

GREEN MORAY EEL

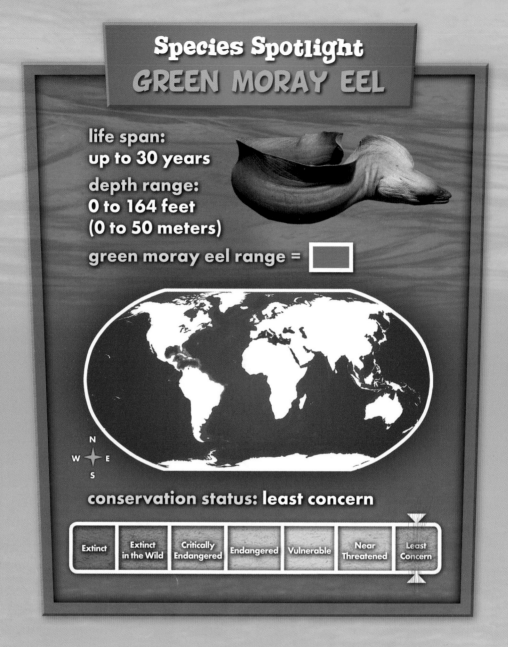

life span:
up to 30 years

depth range:
0 to 164 feet
(0 to 50 meters)

green moray eel range =

conservation status: **least concern**

Extinct	Extinct in the Wild	Critically Endangered	Endangered	Vulnerable	Near Threatened	Least Concern

Eels live in every ocean.
They can often be found along
sandy ocean floors.

Sometimes eels hide in the sand! They also make their homes in **coral reefs** and cracks in rocks.

marbled snake eel

All eels are covered in a slimy **mucus**. This protects them from harmful **parasites**.

These fish also have long fins along their backs. Some have them on their bellies, too. Their fins can be the length of their entire bodies!

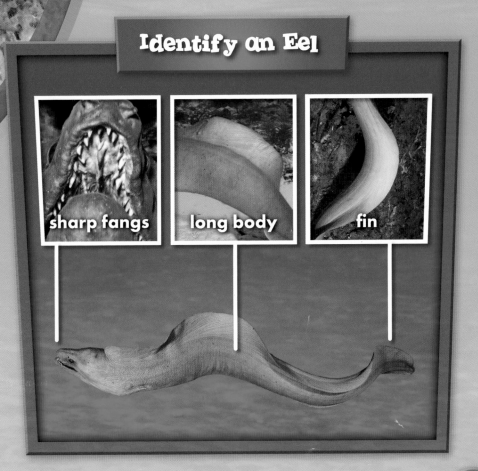

Identify an Eel

sharp fangs

long body

fin

Eels come in many sizes and colors. They range from 4 inches (10.2 centimeters) to more than 11 feet (3.4 meters) long!

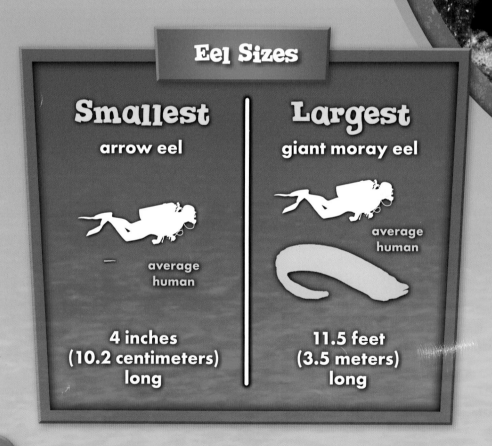

Eel Sizes

Smallest
arrow eel

average human

4 inches
(10.2 centimeters)
long

Largest
giant moray eel

average human

11.5 feet
(3.5 meters)
long

giant
moray eel

Eels found in deep water are often gray or black. **Tropical** eels can be bright and colorful.

Eels open and close their mouths to breathe. This shows off their fearsome fangs!

fangs

mosaic
moray eel

Sharp teeth and strong jaws help eels chew large **prey**. Some eels even have two sets of jaws!

Eels mostly hunt at night. These **carnivores** hide and wait for the perfect snack to swim by.

Then they surprise their prey with a sneak attack! Small fish and crabs are favorite meals.

Catch of the Day

butterfly fish

blue crabs

common octopuses

Sea Enemies

great white sharks

great barracudas

banded sea kraits

These hunters have predators of their own, too. They are no match for hungry barracudas and great white sharks.

Eels stay safe by remaining hidden during the day.

Eels are **solitary** creatures. They spend much of their lives alone in their shelters.

But some eels like to stick
together. Garden eels live
in groups of hundreds!

garden
eels

young
snowflake eel

larvae

Female eels lay thousands of
eggs at once. These eggs turn
into **larvae**.

The larvae float through the water.
They eat **plankton** and grow.
Once their fins are big enough,
they swim off to hunt larger prey!

adult
snowflake eel

Glossary

carnivores—animals that only eat meat

coral reefs—structures made of coral that usually grow in shallow seawater

larvae—early, tiny forms of an eel that must go through a big change to become adults

mucus—a clear liquid that covers the body of an eel

parasites—living things that survive on or in other living things; parasites offer nothing for the food and protection they receive.

plankton—ocean plants or animals that drift in water; most plankton are tiny.

predators—animals that hunt other animals for food

prey—animals that are hunted by other animals for food

slither—to move by smoothly sliding back and forth

solitary—living alone

tropical—related to the tropics; the tropics is a hot region near the equator.

To Learn More

AT THE LIBRARY

Beaton, Kathryn. *Discover Moray Eels*. Ann Arbor, Mich.: Cherry Lake Publishing, 2016.

Duhaime, Darla. *Eels*. Vero Beach, Fla.: Rourke Educational Media, 2017.

Marsh, Laura. *National Geographic Readers: Weird Sea Creatures*. Washington, D.C.: National Geographic, 2012.

ON THE WEB

Learning more about eels is as easy as 1, 2, 3.

1. Go to www.factsurfer.com.

2. Enter "eels" into the search box.

3. Click the "Surf" button and you will see a list of related web sites.

With factsurfer.com, finding more information is just a click away.

Index

The images in this book are reproduced through the courtesy of: Rich Carey, front cover, pp. 4, 16 (top right),
21; AdrianNunez, p. 3; jeffreychin, p. 5; WaterFrame/ Alamy, p. 6; Dray van Beeck, p. 7; Wolfgang Poelzer/
Getty Images, p. 8; eaglerayjoel, p. 9 (top left); Amanda Nicholls, p. 9 (top middle, bottom); Peter Leahy,
p. 9 (top right); Mark Webster/ Getty Images, p. 11; fenkieandreas, p. 12; age fotostock/ SuperStock, p. 13;
Vladimir Wrangel, p. 15 (top left); iusubov nizami, p. 15 (top center); magnusdeepbelow, p. 15 (top right); Ellen
Hui, p. 15; Andrea Izzotti, p. 16 (top left); kaschibo, p. 16 (top center); Michele Westmorland/ Getty Images,
p. 16; Dan Exton, p. 17; Richard Whitcombe, p. 18; Maite Uribarri/ Alamy, p. 19; timsimages, p. 20 (top);
NHPA/ Photoshot/ SuperStock, p. 20 (bottom).